Christ the Lord is Risen Today

(in the style of Beethoven)

"Lyra Davidica"
Arranged by Michele Murray

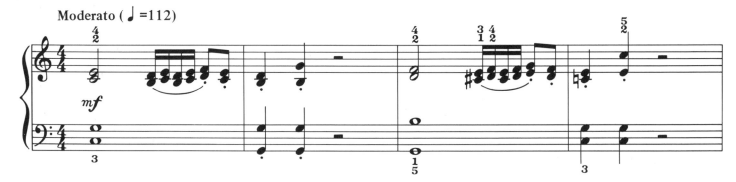

BG0868

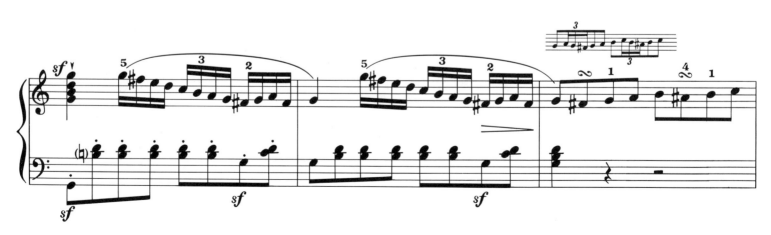

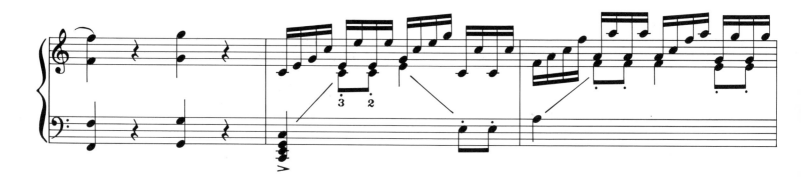

Once in Royal David's City

(in the style of Bach)

Henry J. Gauntlett
Arranged by Michele Murray

BG0868

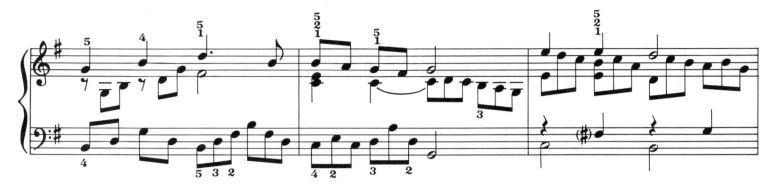

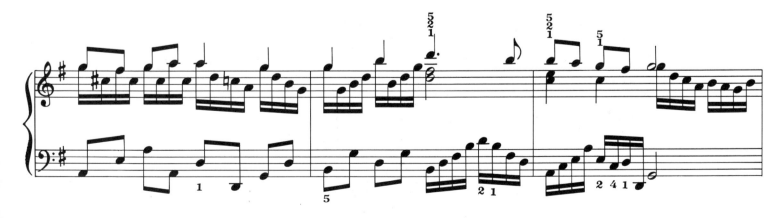

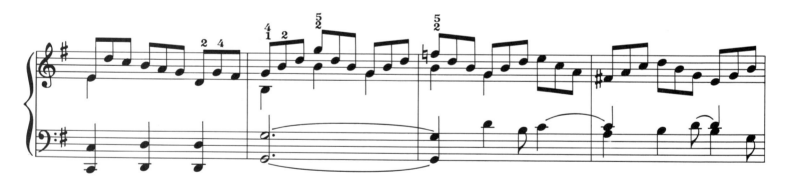

Christmas Medley

(in the style of Schumann)

Adeste Fidelis/Greensleeves/In Dulci Jubilo
Arranged by Michele Murray

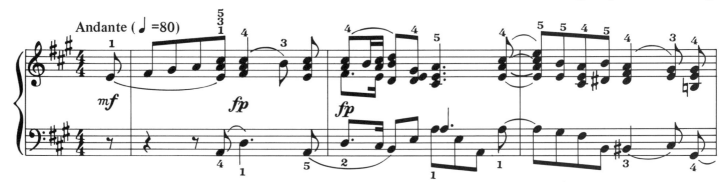

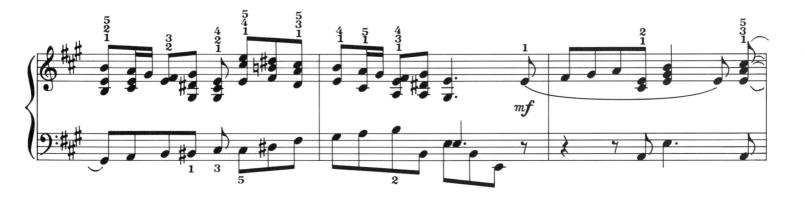

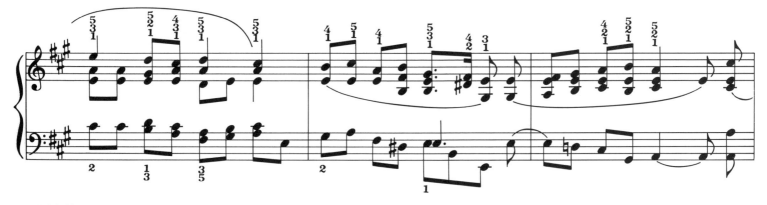

BG0868

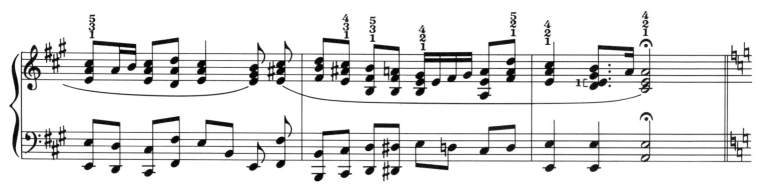

Allegretto (♩=126)

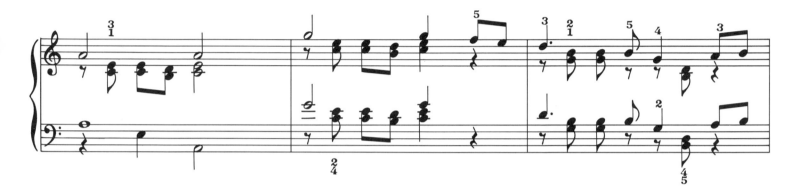

Lento (♪ = 116)

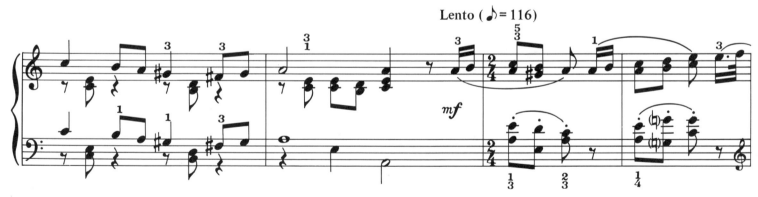

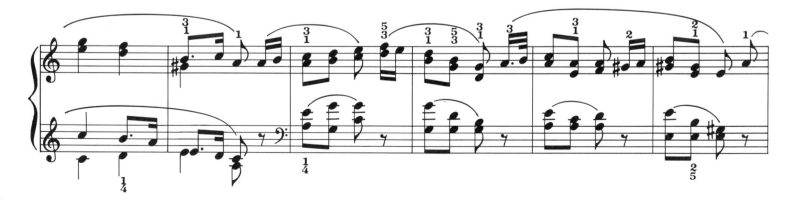

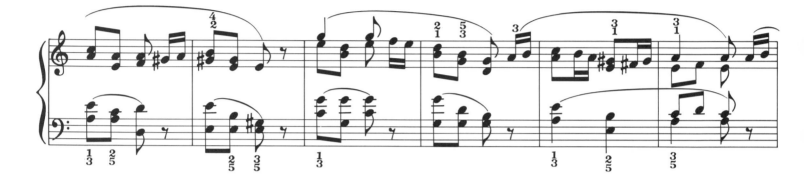

Moderato (♩.=108)

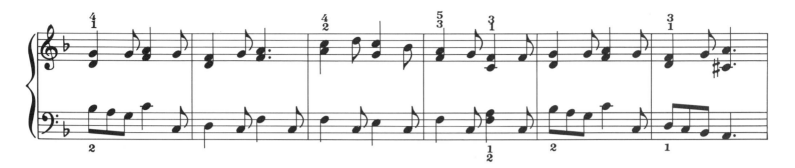

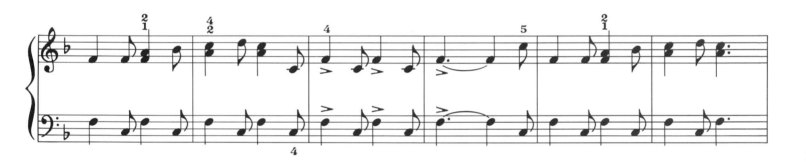

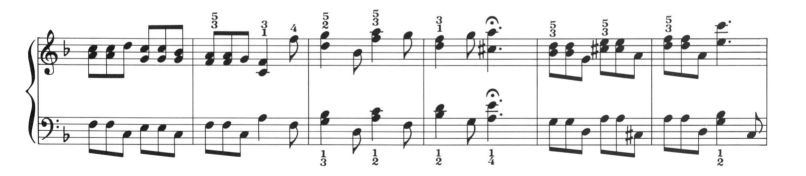

The Old Rugged Cross

(in the style of Liszt)

George Bennard
Arranged by Michele Murray

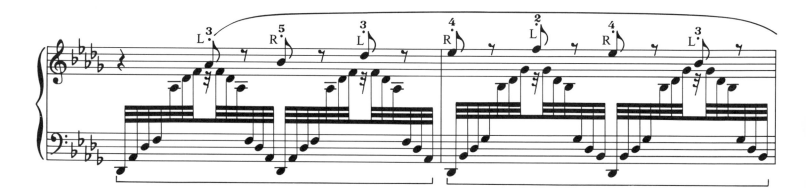

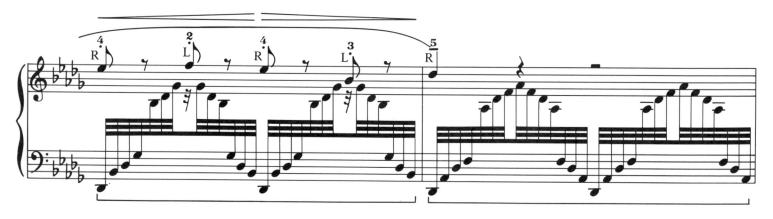

BG0868

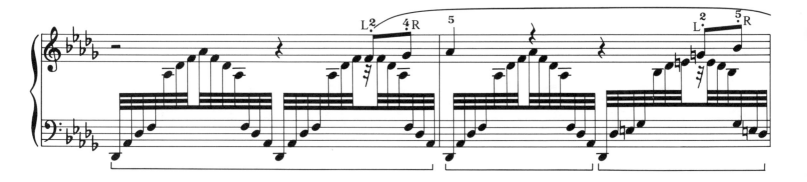

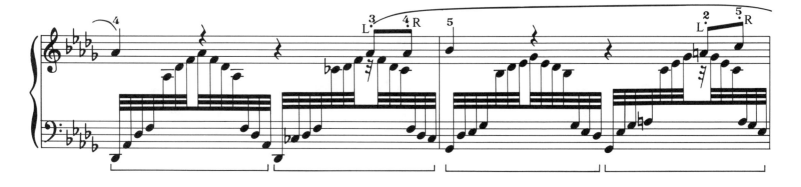

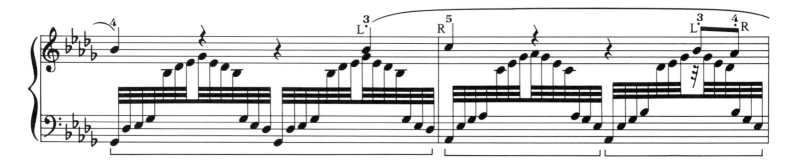

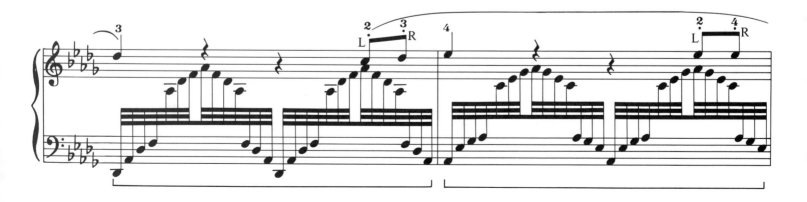

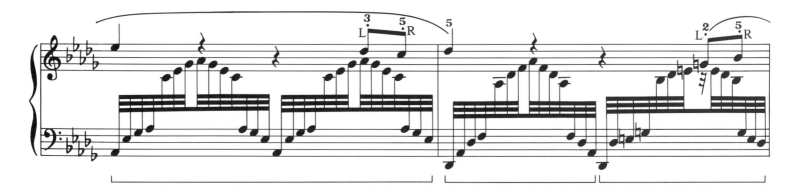

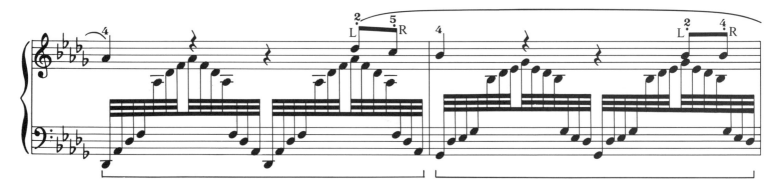

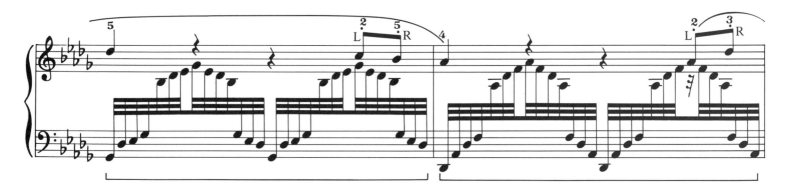

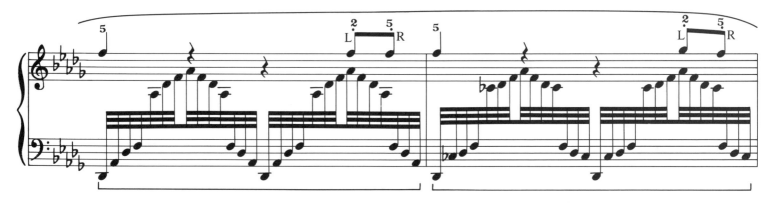

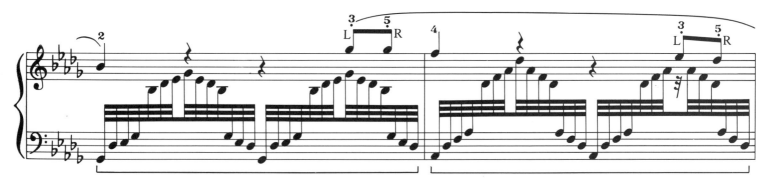

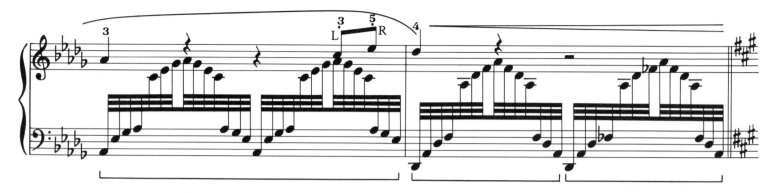

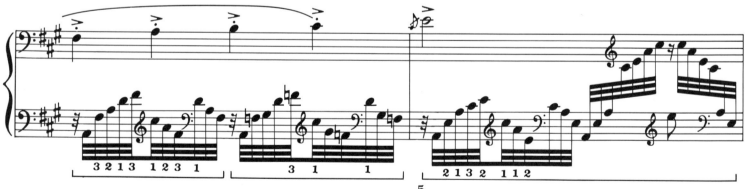

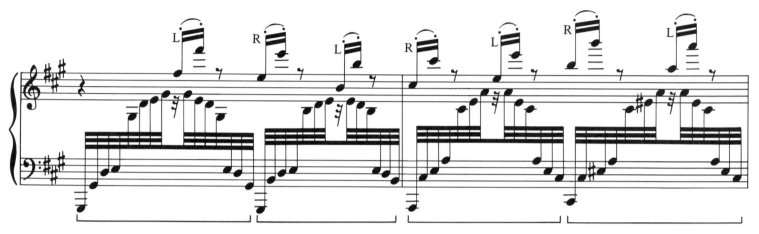

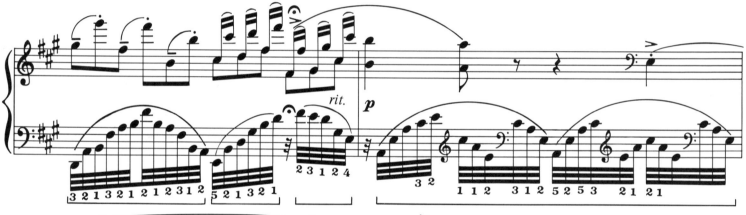

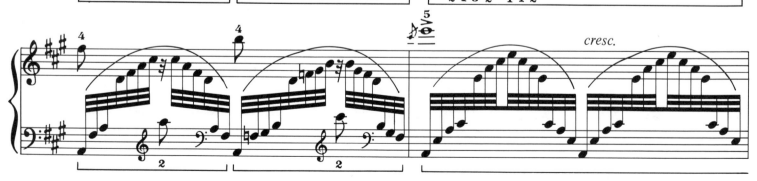

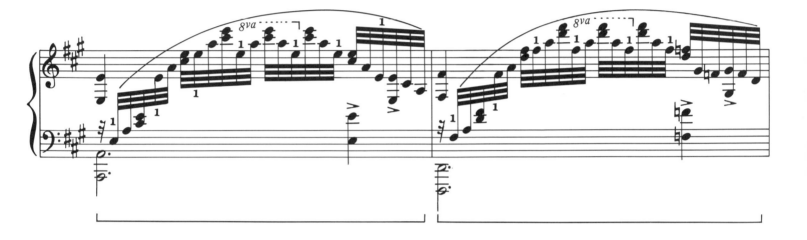

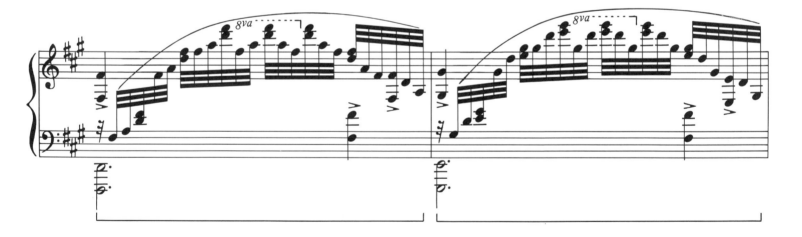

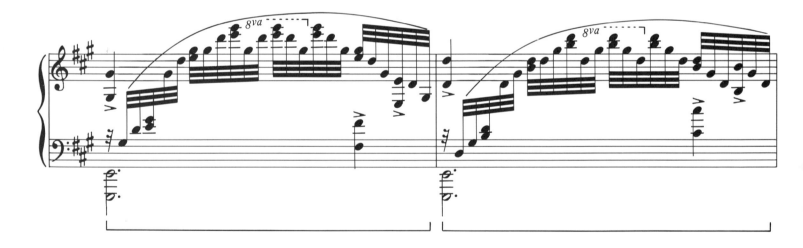

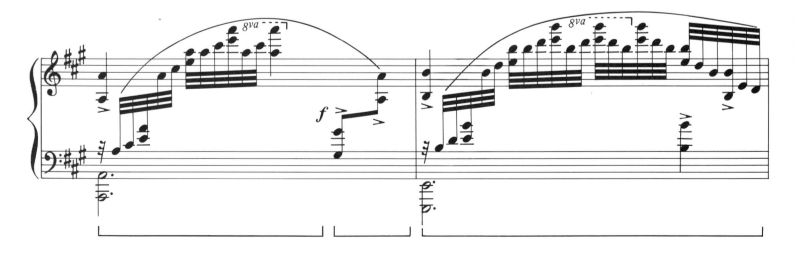

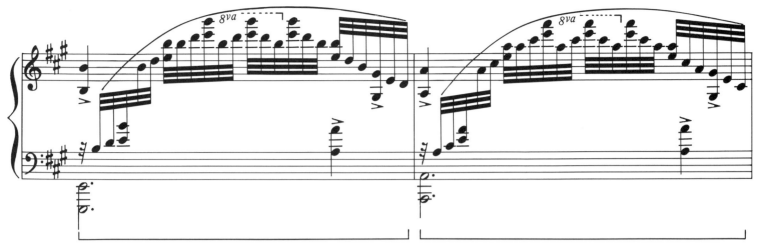

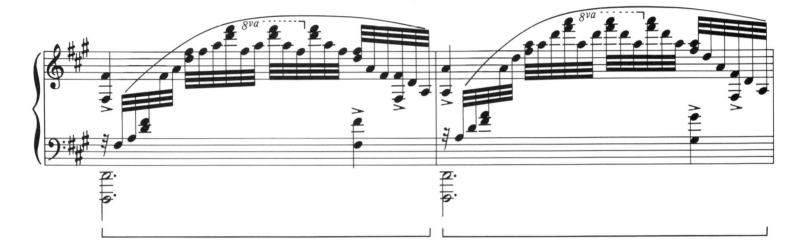

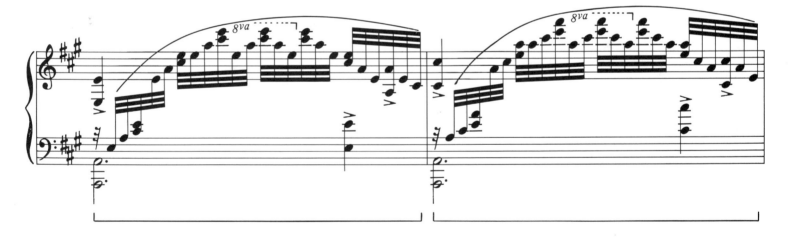

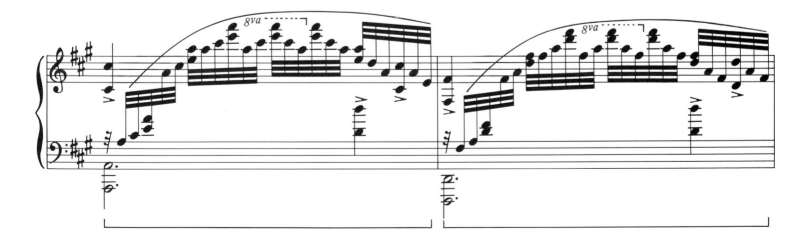

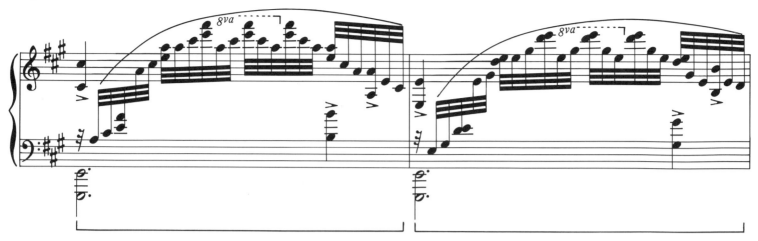

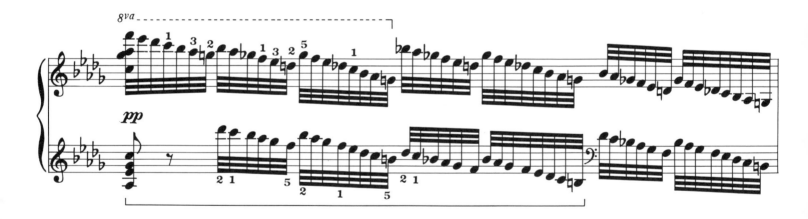

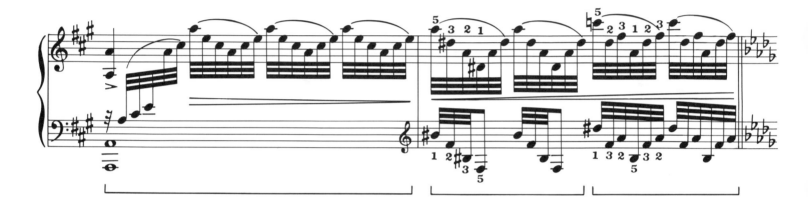

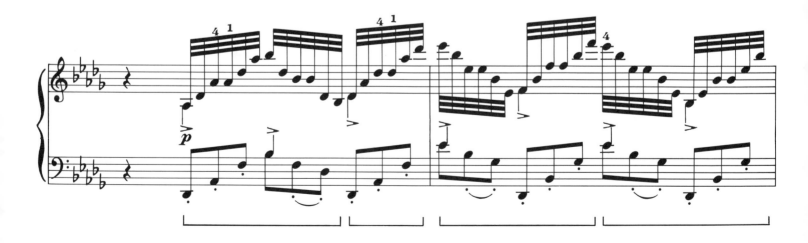

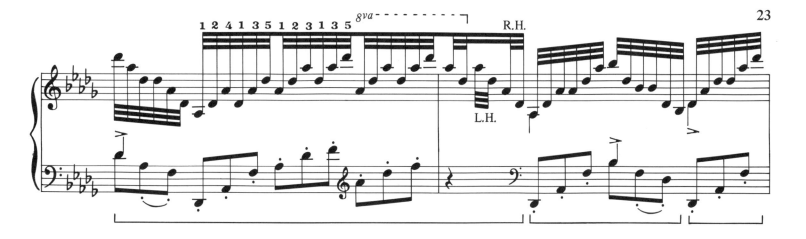

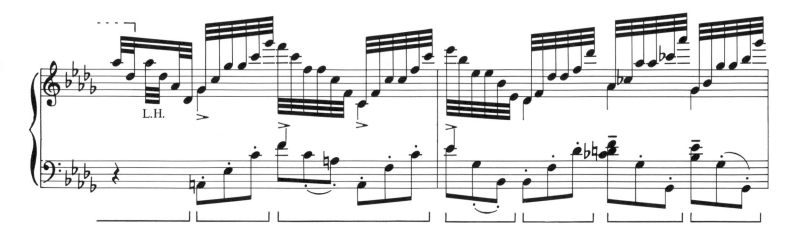

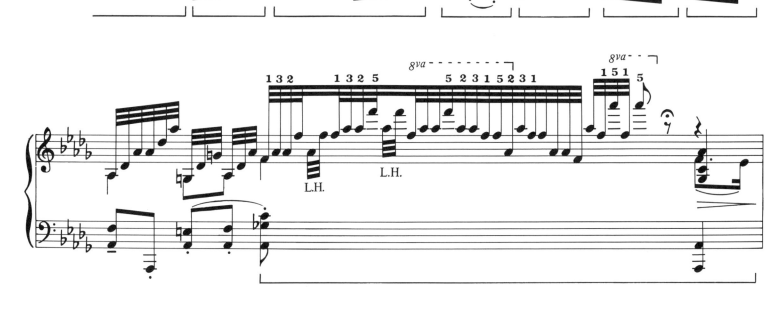

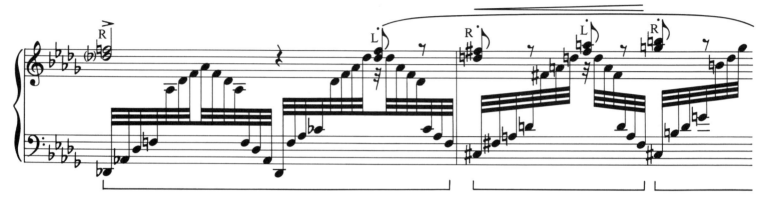

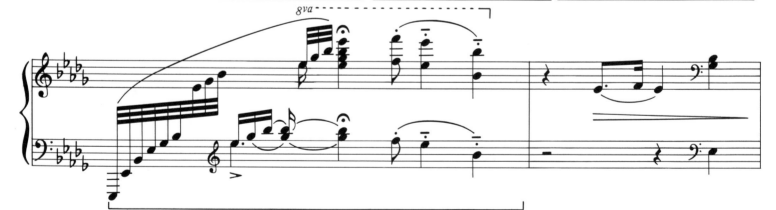

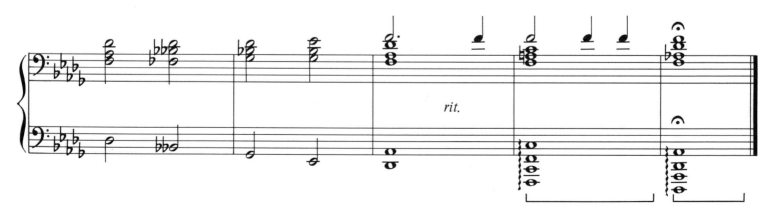

Battle Hymn of the Republic

(in the style of Schubert)

American Melody
Arranged by Michele Murray

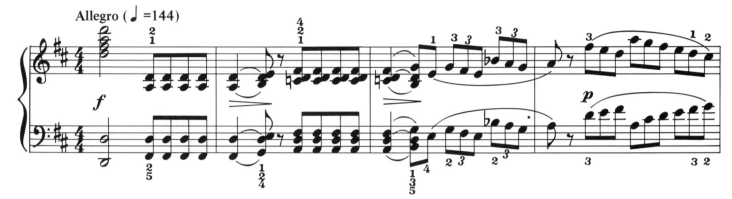

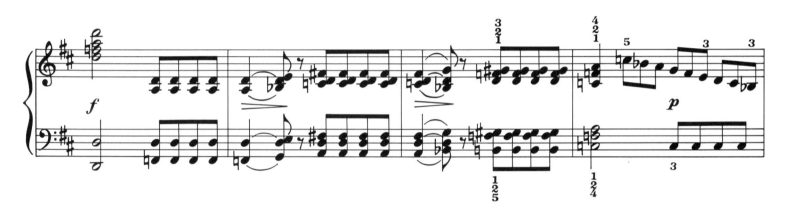

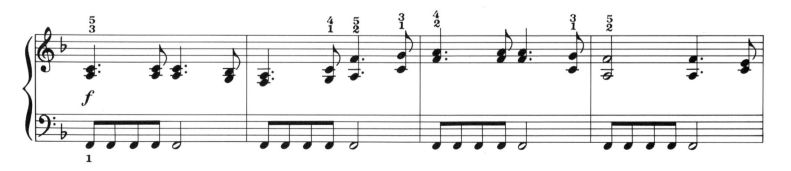

BG0868

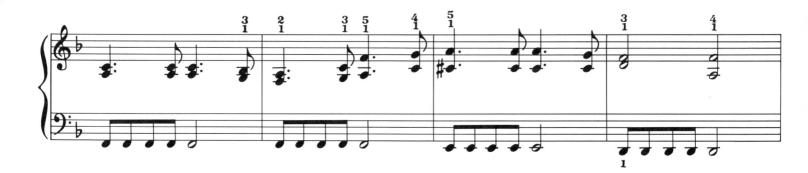

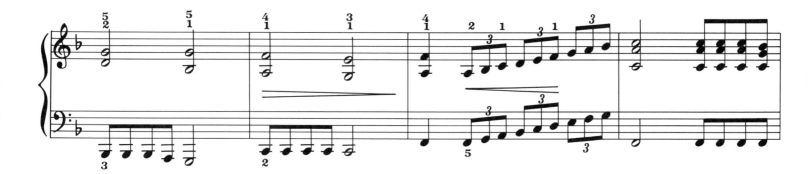

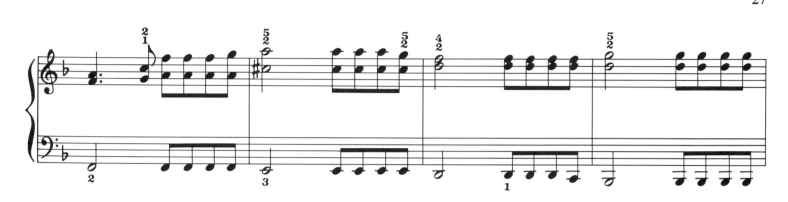

28

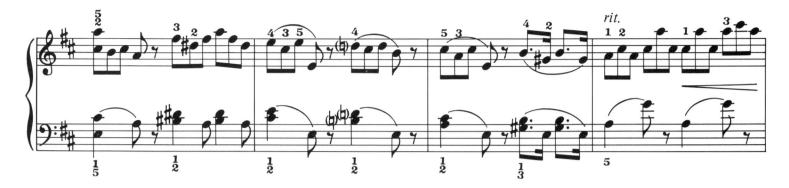

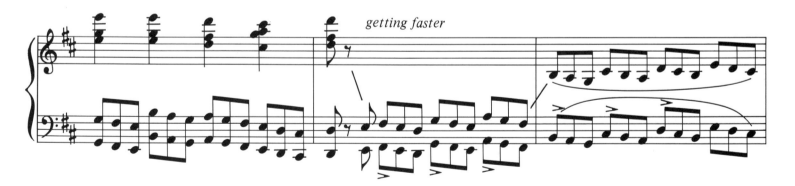

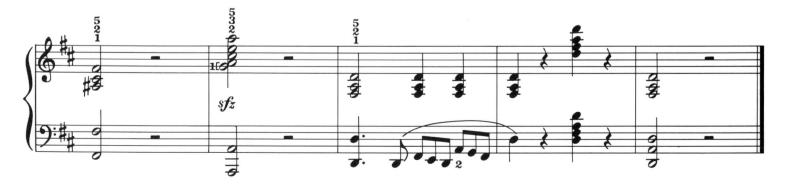

We Gather Together

(in the style of MacDowell)

Netherlands Folk Song
Arranged by Michele Murray

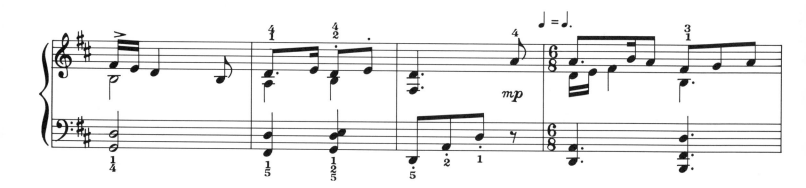

BG0868

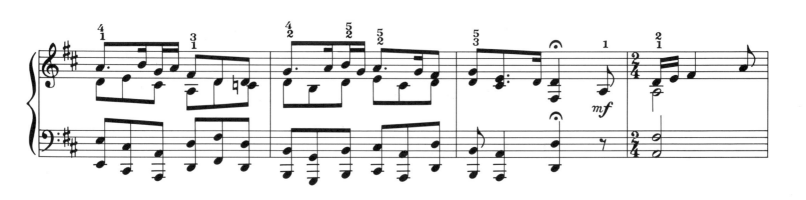

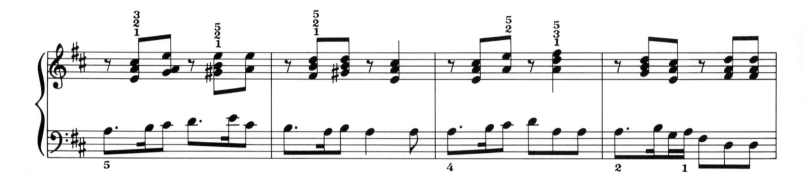

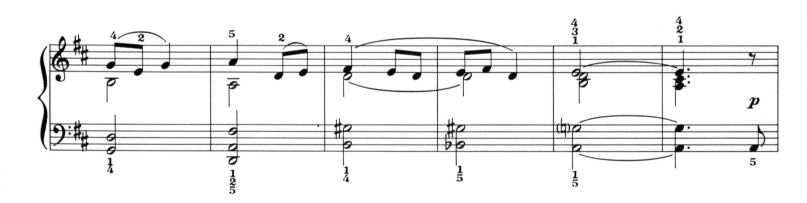

Turn Your Eyes Upon Jesus

(in the style of Brahms)

Helen H. Lemmel
Arranged by Michele Murray

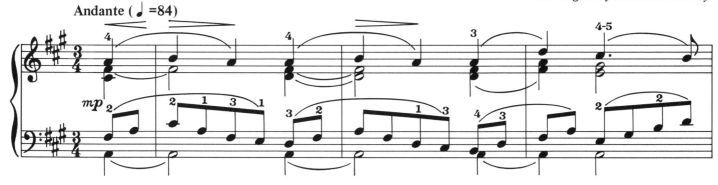

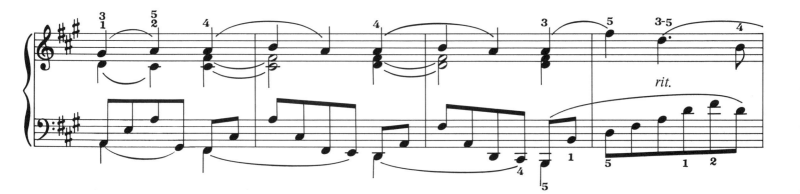

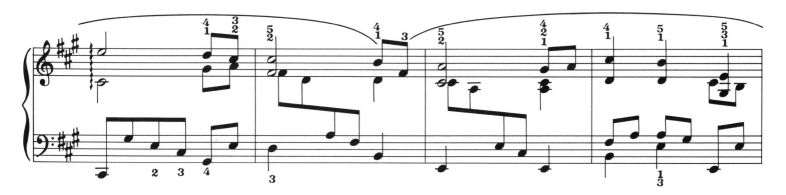

BG0868

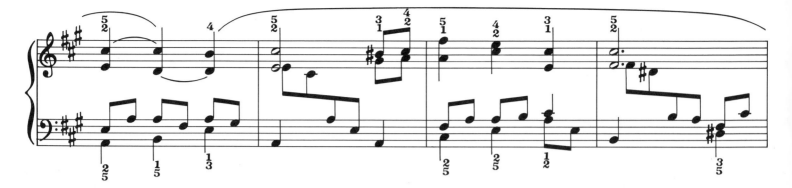

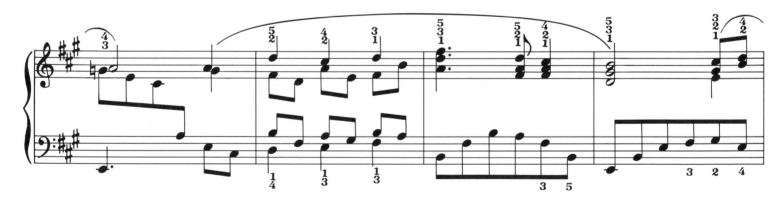

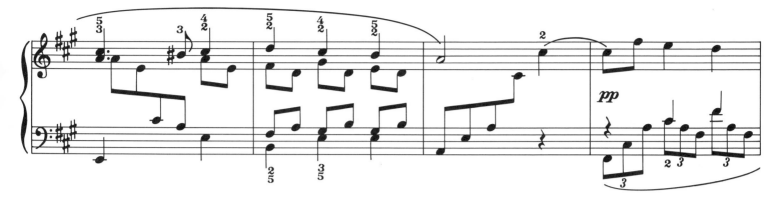

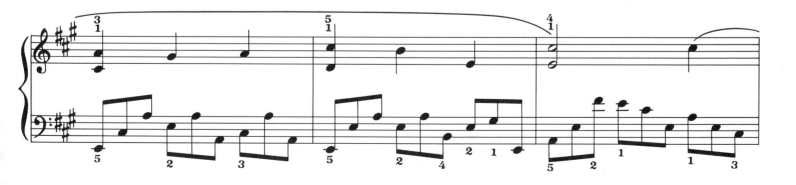

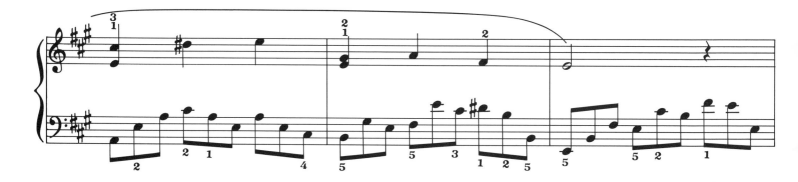

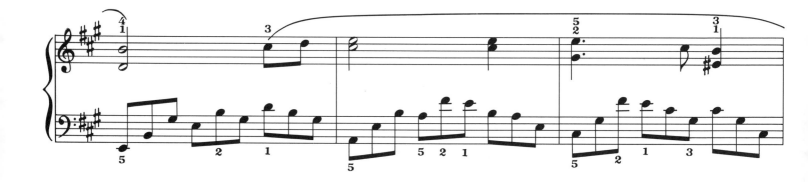

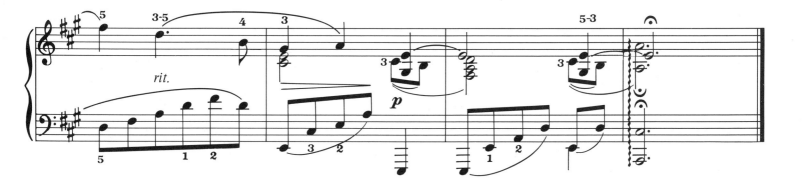

Patriotic Medley

(in the style of Bach)

Henry Carey / Samuel A. Ward
Arranged by Michele Murray

BG0868

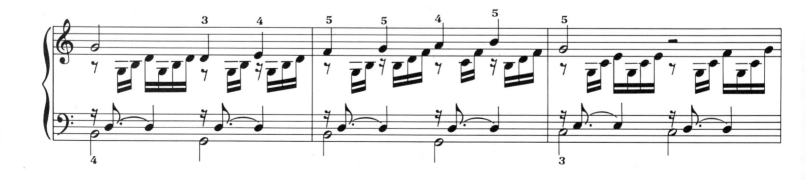